ERWOMEN in STEM

Women Scientists in Life Science

NANCY DICKMANN

Gareth Stevens
PUBLISHING

Please visit our website, www.garethstevens.com.
For a free color catalog of all our high-quality books,
call toll-free 1-800-542-2595 or fax 1-877-542-2596.

Cataloging-in-Publication Data
Names: Dickmann, Nancy.
Title: Women scientists in life science / Nancy Dickmann.
Description: New York : Gareth Stevens Publishing, 2018. | Series: Superwomen in STEM | Includes index.
Identifiers: LCCN ISBN 9781538214718 (pbk.) | ISBN 9781538214060 (library bound) | ISBN 9781538214725 (6 pack)
Subjects: LCSH: Women in science--Juvenile literature. | Women scientists--Juvenile literature.
Classification: LCC Q130.D53 2018 | DDC 305.43'5--dc23

Published in 2018 by
Gareth Stevens Publishing
111 East 14th Street, Suite 349
New York, NY 10003

Copyright © 2018 Brown Bear Books Ltd

For Brown Bear Books Ltd:
Text and Editor: Nancy Dickmann
Designer and Illustrator: Supriya Sahai
Editorial Director: Lindsey Lowe
Children's Publisher: Anne O'Daly
Design Manager: Keith Davis
Picture Manager: Sophie Mortimer
Concept development: Square and Circus / Brown Bear Books Ltd

Picture Credits: Cover: Illustrations of women: Supriya Sahai. All icons Shutterstock. Alamy: ClassicStock 27, RosaIreneBetancourt9 17, Liam
White 33; istockphoto: almintang 14, asiseeit 5, kickstand 20, sochAnam 26, Elm Villa 8; Library of Congress: 28; NOAA Photo Library: 40;
NobelPrize.org: 23; Public Domain: 32, 35, 41, National Geographic Voices 38, OAR/National Undersea Research Program 39, Philosophical
Transactions of the Royal Society/Everard Horne 9, Sedgwick Museum 11, University of Wyoming 4; Shutterstock: 29, Roger Costa Morera 22,
Lefteris Papaulakis 10, Rost9 21; Thinkstock: istockphoto 16, 34, Rom Rodinka 15.

Character artwork © Supriya Sahai
All other artwork Brown Bear Books Ltd

Brown Bear Books has made every attempt to contact the copyright holders.
If anyone has any information please contact licensing@brownbearbooks.co.uk

Manufactured in the United States of America

CPSIA compliance information: Batch #CW18GS. For further information contact Gareth Stevens, New York, New York at 1-800-542-2595.

Contents

The Science of Life

From thick forests to the ocean depths, living things are everywhere. Scientists have made amazing discoveries about how life began, and how it has changed over time.

The study of life sciences is divided into many branches. Zoologists study animals, while botanists study plants. Paleontologists study living things that died out many thousands of years ago. Some scientists focus on particular aspects of life, such as the geneticists who study the way that traits are passed down from parents to offspring.

Studying the remains of extinct animals helps us to understand how living things change over time.

Today, girls and women are able to study whatever subjects they want.

PUTTING IT ALL TOGETHER

Living things exist in ecosystems—networks of plants and animals that are dependent on each other. If one species declines, others in the ecosystem can be affected. In recent years, scientists have realized how important this balance is. Dedicated scientists study the effects of change on ecosystems, and conservationists work to protect the natural world.

MAKING THEIR MARK

For many years, women had to fight to be recognized as scientists. They were not allowed to study at universities, and were not expected to be interested in science. However, many women began to study the natural world as a hobby. They made observations, researched the work of other scientists, and drew their own conclusions. Although it often took years for them to be taken seriously, these trailblazers paved the way for a new generation of women scientists. Today, many of the world's top scientists are women.

Mary Anning

Mary Anning came from humble beginnings, but she made discoveries that helped some of the world's greatest scientists prove their theories.

Mary was one of ten children born to Richard and Molly Anning in the town of Lyme Regis. Richard worked making furniture, but the family was poor. Most of Mary's siblings died young—only she and her brother Joseph survived to adulthood. In fact, Mary almost didn't make it. One day while she was still a toddler, a neighbor took Mary to watch a horse show. They took shelter under a tree with two other women during a storm. Suddenly lightning struck the tree, killing all three adults, but little Mary survived.

QUICK FACTS

NAME: Mary Anning

BIRTH: 1799, Lyme Regis, England

OCCUPATION: Fossil collector and paleontologist

EDUCATION: Self-taught

SELLING "CURIOS"

Lyme Regis is on the southern coast of England, and its cliffs date back to the Jurassic period. As the cliffs wore away and collapsed, fossils were revealed. Richard Anning earned extra money for his family by finding fossils and selling them to tourists, who called them "curios." He taught Mary how to find and clean fossils for sale. When Richard died in 1810, Mary and Joseph tried to support the family by hunting for fossils.

ICHTHYOSAUR

In 1811, Joseph found a 4-foot (1.2 m) long skull of a crocodile-like creature. A few months later, Mary uncovered the rest of the skeleton. At the age of 12, she had discovered the most complete ichthyosaur ever found. It was later displayed in a museum.

The cliffs at Lyme Regis are still a popular spot for fossil hunters.

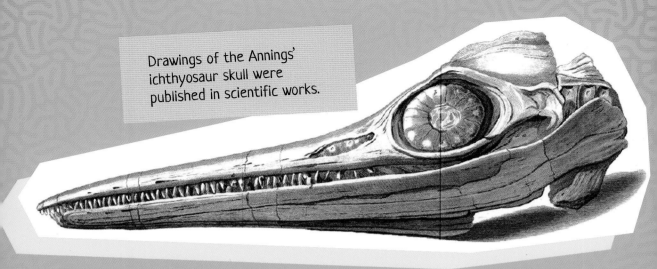

Drawings of the Annings' ichthyosaur skull were published in scientific works.

A scientist wrote a paper about it, but he gave the Annings no credit. Science was seen as something for the upper classes, not for uneducated fossil hunters like Mary.

CHANGING IDEAS

In the early 1800s, most people in England still believed in the version of history provided by the Bible, which implied that the planet was only a few thousand years old. They believed that living things had not changed during this time. Discoveries like Mary's ichthyosaur challenged this belief. The creatures were obviously like nothing that existed on Earth. Could Earth be older than everyone thought?

MORE FINDS

Mary had become friends with an older woman, Elizabeth Philpot, who went fossil hunting with her. It could be dangerous work—one day a sudden landslide killed Mary's dog, and almost killed Mary too.

Mary and her fossil business became well-known. She is the subject of the famous tongue twister "She sells seashells by the seashore."

❝ She says the world has used her ill... these men of learning have sucked her brains, and made a great deal of publishing works, of which she furnished the contents, while she derived [gained] none of the advantages. ❞

A friend of Mary Anning

A GROWING REPUTATION

Mary continued to find impressive fossils, and her reputation spread. In 1823 she discovered the first complete skeleton of a plesiosaurus. Five years later, she found a type of winged reptile called a pterosaur—the first one ever found in England. Despite these finds, she and her family remained poor.

SHUT OUT

Many scientists came to Lyme Regis, and Mary sometimes led them on fossil-hunting trips. Her discoveries formed the basis of many scientific papers and theories. She even suggested to one scientist, William Buckland, that the "stones" found in ichthyosaur skeletons might actually be fossilized feces.

But while many men scientists respected her skills, they did not see her as an equal. They treated her differently because she was a woman, and because she came from a lower class.

In the years since Mary's original discovery, many other plesiosaurus skeletons have been found.

With her basket, rock hammer, and faithful dog, Mary was a familiar sight near the cliffs of Lyme Regis.

ALWAYS LEARNING

Mary remained determined to be more than just a fossil hunter. She read everything she could find on paleontology. Sometimes she would add her own suggestions and amendments to what she read. She wrote and received letters from important scientists, and was eventually recognized as an expert in her field.

DEATH AND LEGACY

Mary was diagnosed with breast cancer in 1845. At that time there was no effective treatment for it. She died two years later, at the age of just 47. Both before and after her death, several species of animal were named for her. In 2010, the UK's top science organization named her as one of the ten British women who have most influenced the history of science.

Marjory
Stoneman Douglas

Marjory Stoneman Douglas was a writer who used her skills in the interest of science. She loved the Florida Everglades and worked hard to protect them.

Marjory was born in Minnesota in 1890 and moved to Massachusetts with her mother six years later, when her parents separated. Marjory loved reading and writing, and at the age of 16 she had an article published in a magazine. Relatives saved up to send her to Wellesley College, where she majored in English. She made many good friends at Wellesley, and she joined a club that fought for women's right to vote.

QUICK FACTS

NAME: Marjory Stoneman Douglas

BIRTH: 1890, Minneapolis, Minnesota

OCCUPATION: Writer and conservationist

EDUCATION: Wellesley College

> 66 There are no other Everglades in the world. They are, they have always been, one of the unique regions of the earth; remote, never wholly known. Nothing anywhere else is like them. 99

FINDING HER WAY

Shortly after Marjory's graduation in 1912, her mother died from breast cancer. Marjory wasn't quite sure what to do next, so she moved to St. Louis to live with one of her college friends and took a job in a department store. Later she moved to New Jersey, where she met Kenneth Douglas. He was 30 years older than her, and claimed to be a newspaper editor. They got married, but Kenneth was not what he seemed. After little more than a year of marriage, Marjory left him and moved to Florida in 1915 to live with her father. She hadn't seen him since she was a child.

Marjory was happy at Wellesley, where she edited the yearbook.

The Everglades are famous for their natural beauty, but in the past many people saw them as a worthless swamp.

NEWSPAPER CAREER

Marjory's father was an editor for the *Miami Herald* newspaper, and he offered her a job. She started on the society page, reporting on tea parties and dances.

After traveling to France to work for the Red Cross during World War I (1914–1918), she returned to the *Herald*. Marjory became an assistant editor, and wrote editorials as well as her own daily column. She applied her strong opinions and sharp wit to any topic she chose. She was already starting to take an interest in conservation. One of the areas she was particularly interested in was the Everglades, a large area of wetlands near Miami.

The Everglades cover a large area of southern Florida. A very shallow river up to 50 miles (80 km) wide flows slowly through the park, on its way south to the coast. Much of it is covered with a plant called saw grass. The area is a haven for wading birds and other animals such as alligators and turtles.

"When she spoke, everybody stopped slapping (mosquitoes) and more or less came to order. She reminded us all of our responsibility to nature..."

Marjory's friend
John Rothchild

RIVER OF GRASS

In 1942, Marjory began research for a book about the Everglades. Five years later, *The Everglades: River of Grass* was published. It changed the way many people thought about the region by describing its wildlife and natural beauty. The book also explored the way that dams and drainage systems in the past had damaged the delicate ecosystem.

REACTION TO THE BOOK

The book was well received by the critics. Marjory had applied her journalistic skills to a scientific topic, and the result was a book that was well-written but with a strong message. Interest in conserving the Everglades grew as a result of *River of Grass*. In 1947, the year it was published, Everglades National Park was opened. However, it only included part of the region. There was still work to do.

About one million people visit Everglades National Park each year to see the unique wildlife.

Marjory was famous for her trademark hat, and for her strong opinions!

FIGHTING FOR THE EVERGLADES

Engineers regularly build dams and levees to control the flow of rivers and prevent flooding. But doing this was cutting off water to the Everglades, damaging the ecosystem. In the late 1960s, construction began on what was planned to be an enormous airport there. Marjory knew that this would destroy wildlife. She founded the Friends of the Everglades, a group that would fight to protect the region.

AWARDS AND HONORS

Marjory lived to the age of 108, and she never stopped fighting to protect the Everglades. For her 100th birthday, she asked that people plant trees instead of giving her gifts. President Bill Clinton awarded her the Presidential Medal of Freedom, the nation's highest civilian honor. Perhaps the most fitting tribute came the year before she died, when a section of the park that she loved so much was named for her.

Barbara McClintock

Who we are is down to what's in our genes. Barbara McClintock made discoveries that changed our view of genes forever.

In 1902, Thomas and Sara McClintock's third child was born. It was a girl and they named her Eleanor. However, they soon decided that Eleanor was a gentle, feminine name, while their daughter was anything but! They started to call her Barbara, which they thought suited her no-nonsense personality better. She would be "Barbara" for the rest of her life. As a child, Barbara was independent and loved being on her own. Her parents encouraged her to be the person she wanted to be, and to do what made her happy.

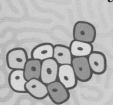

QUICK FACTS

NAME: Eleanor "Barbara" McClintock

BIRTH: 1902, Hartford, Connecticut

OCCUPATION: Botanist and geneticist

EDUCATION: Cornell University

> **If you know you are on the right track, if you have this inner knowledge, then nobody can turn you off... no matter what they say.**

COLLEGE

Barbara was a bright child, and her high school teachers encouraged her to think about going to college—maybe even becoming a professor one day. At that time, not many women went to college. Barbara's mother was against it—she thought it would spoil her chances of getting married. But Barbara's father supported her, and she went to Cornell University to study botany and genetics.

CYTOGENETICS

Barbara stayed at Cornell to get a master's degree and then a PhD. Her research was in an area called cytogenetics. It focuses on how genes relate to a cell's behavior, especially during the process when a cell divides in two.

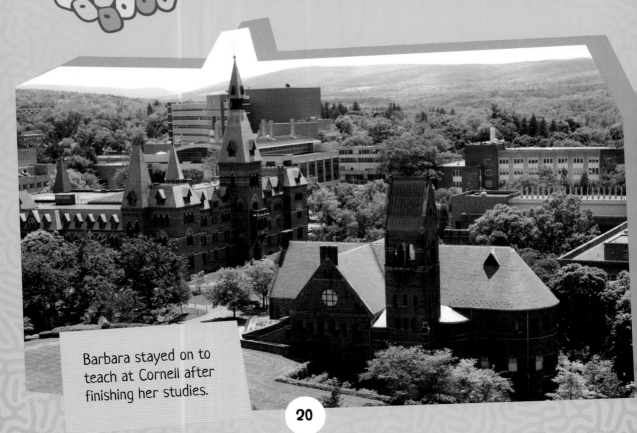

Barbara stayed on to teach at Cornell after finishing her studies.

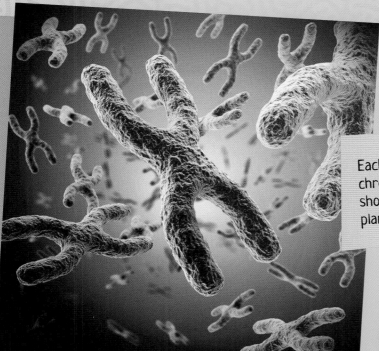

Each human cell has 46 chromosomes like the ones shown here. Most maize plants have 20.

Barbara studied the genes of the corn plant, often called maize. She used microscopes to see inside cells. She also grew corn plants, to investigate how the cellular changes affected the growing plants.

CHROMOSOME CROSSOVER

Barbara's first major discovery was that individual genes could swap between one chromosome and another. This idea had been suggested 20 years earlier, but no one had been able to prove it. Barbara developed new techniques that let her see chromosomes under a microscope better than anyone had before. Her findings proved the theory.

Genes carry instructions that control a living thing's physical features. In each cell, genetic material is arranged into structures called chromosomes. During reproduction, chromosomes split and make copies of themselves. This is how genes get passed on from one generation to the next.

> 66 **I was just so interested in what I was doing I could hardly wait to get up in the morning and get at it. One of my friends, a geneticist, said I was a child, because only children can't wait to get up in the morning to get at what they want to do.** 99

CHANGING JOBS

In 1936, Barbara moved to the University of Missouri and started working with X-rays. She was investigating how they caused unexpected changes called mutations in chromosomes. Six years later, she accepted a job at Cold Spring Harbor Laboratory in Long Island, New York. She would no longer have to teach and could focus on research instead. She would stay there for the rest of her career.

AHEAD OF HER TIME

In the 1940s, Barbara started to research the link between a corn plant's color and its chromosomes. She discovered that genes could change more quickly than anyone realized. Her research was ahead of its time. It received little interest from other scientists, and although she kept researching, she stopped publishing her work.

A corn plant's genes cause variations, such as different colors.

"JUMPING GENES"

Barbara discovered the gene changes by comparing one plant's chromosomes to those of its parent plant. They should have been identical, but to her surprise, some of the genes in the offspring were in different positions. It was like they had been snipped out and moved somewhere else—almost as though they had jumped!

NOBEL PRIZE

It wasn't until the 1960s and 1970s that other scientists began to confirm Barbara's discoveries. Awards and prizes soon followed, including the National Medal of Science. In 1983, she was awarded the Nobel Prize in Physiology or Medicine for her work on genes. She died in 1992, at the age of 90.

Presenting her research to the Nobel Prize Committee in 1983 was one of the great moments in Barbara's life.

Rachel Carson

Communicating new discoveries to the public is an important job. Rachel Carson drew attention to the problem of pollution — and she started a revolution.

Rachel had a happy childhood with her older brother and sister. Her father was an insurance salesman. Money was tight, but her family's home was surrounded by acres of countryside. Rachel's mother loved to read and spend time outdoors, and she passed these hobbies on to her children. Rachel always knew she wanted to be a writer, but she was also interested in learning about nature.

QUICK FACTS

NAME: Rachel Louise Carson

BIRTH: 1907, Springdale, Pennsylvania

OCCUPATION: Marine biologist and author

EDUCATION: Chatham University, Johns Hopkins University

GOING TO COLLEGE

Rachel was a good student, and she won two scholarships to a women's college in Pittsburgh, not too far from her home. Her family struggled to pay her living expenses, so Rachel made sure to work hard to make their sacrifices worth it. She started as an English major, but she did so well in a biology class that her teacher persuaded her to switch majors. Rachel graduated in 1929 near the top of her class.

Rachel was awarded a scholarship for a master's degree program at Johns Hopkins University. She also began doing hands-on research in marine biology. After finishing her master's degree, she began working on a PhD, but money was still a problem. Rachel had to give up her studies to help support her family.

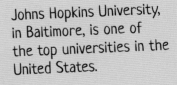

Johns Hopkins University, in Baltimore, is one of the top universities in the United States.

Before owning a television became common, most people listened to the radio for entertainment.

GOVERNMENT WORKER

Rachel needed a job, so she turned back to her childhood dream of being a writer. She eventually found a job with the US Bureau of Fisheries, writing scripts for radio programs about wildlife. She had a gift for making science topics interesting and accessible for the general public.

PROFESSIONAL WRITER

Rachel was asked to write a book about marine life. She had to fit her writing time around her full-time job. She also went on research trips whenever she could. Her first book didn't sell well, but her second became a best seller. Rachel became recognized and respected—and she was able to quit her job to concentrate on her writing.

Some of Rachel's magazine articles appeared under the name "R. L. Carson." She and her editors thought that her work would be taken more seriously if people didn't know it had been written by a woman.

> **❝ [I believe in] the right of the citizen to be secure in his own home against the intrusion of poisons applied by other persons… I strongly feel that this is or should be one of the basic human rights. ❞**

SILENT SPRING

In the 1950s, Rachel began research for a book on pesticides. These chemicals helped farmers by killing insects, but no one had studied their effects on humans and wildlife. Some of the pesticides were killing birds as well as insects. Rachel called the book *Silent Spring*, because in some communities, so many birds had been killed by pesticides that in spring, the normal chorus of birdsong was absent.

MAKING AN IMPACT

Silent Spring caused controversy as soon as it was published. Chemical manufacturers were worried that the book would lead to a ban on the pesticides that brought them millions of dollars. They attacked Rachel's research and tried to discredit her.

In the 1950s, airplanes called "crop dusters" sprayed pesticides over large areas of farmland.

Thanks to new anti-pollution laws, birds returned to areas where they had been in decline.

CHANGING THE LAWS

However, Rachel's research had been thorough. Several respected scientists spoke up in support of her book. Rachel testified before the US Senate to argue for stronger anti-pollution laws. Conservation charities sprang up, inspired by *Silent Spring*. President Nixon set up the Environmental Protection Agency, and stronger pollution laws were soon passed.

LASTING LEGACY

Sadly, Rachel didn't live to see the full impact of her work. She had been diagnosed with breast cancer while writing the book, and she died in 1964 at the age of just 56. But her work had a real impact, and inspired a new generation of conservationists. A wildlife refuge in the Maine wilderness that she loved so much is now named for her.

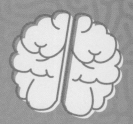

Dian Fossey

Dian Fossey was an unconventional zoologist. She devoted her life to studying and protecting African mountain gorillas.

Dian's work on gorilla behavior changed the popular view of gorillas as being brutal animals, showing them instead to be peaceful animals living in family groups. Born on January 16, 1932, Dian had a difficult childhood. Her parents divorced when she was six, and her stepfather was very strict. Dian found comfort in being with animals. She wanted to be a vet and began studying pre-veterinary science at the University of California. But Dian struggled with the chemistry in the course and failed in her second year.

QUICK FACTS

NAME: Dian Fossey

BIRTH: 1932, San Francisco, California

OCCUPATION: Zoologist

EDUCATION: San Jose State College, University of Cambridge

Biruté Galdikas, Jane Goodall, and Dian Fossey studied primates in their natural environments. They studied orangutans, chimpanzees, and gorillas, and were often called "The Trimates"!

66 When you realize the value of all life, you dwell less on what is past and concentrate more on the preservation of the future. 99

OCCUPATIONAL THERAPY

Dian transferred to San Jose State College to study occupational therapy. She worked in hospitals in California and then moved to Louisville, Kentucky, in 1955 to join the Kosair Crippled Children's Hospital.

DREAMS OF AFRICA

Dian dreamed of going to Africa to work with animals. In 1963, she borrowed some money and used her life savings to fund a six-week trip there. While she was in Africa, Dian met famous anthropologists Mary Leakey and her husband Louis Leakey. He told her about the work of another woman scientist—Jane Goodall—who was engaged in a long-term study of chimpanzees in the wild.

Dian went back to Africa in 1966. She had seen wild mountain gorillas on her first trip. She was determined to study them, in their natural habitat, in the same way that Jane Goodall was studying chimpanzees.

"THE WOMAN WHO LIVES ALONE"

Mountain gorillas lived in the mountain forests on either side of the border between Congo and Rwanda. Dian began her studies in the Congo. Political unrest made it dangerous to stay there, so she had to relocate to Rwanda.

On September 24, 1967, Dian set up camp in a part of the rain forest between two volcanoes: Mt. Karisimbi and Mt. Visoke. She named the camp Karisoke, taking the name from the two volcanoes. The local people called her Nyirmachabelli, or "The woman who lives alone on the mountain."

Dian Fossey wrote a book about her life and work with the gorillas. The book, *Gorillas in the Mist*, was turned into a movie starring Sigourney Weaver.

Dian Fossey grew very close to some of the gorillas that she studied.

" Gorillas are almost altruistic in nature. When I get back to civilization, I'm always appalled by 'me, me, me.' "

STUDYING GORILLAS

Gorillas are shy, and they live in dense forests, so the first step in studying them was finding them! With the help of local trackers, Dian soon learned to spot signs of gorillas and follow them. At first, gorillas fled as soon as they saw someone watching them. But over time, they got used to Dian's presence. She often copied their behaviors such as scratching and walking with her knuckles on the ground, which helped them accept her.

Life in the mountains was challenging. The wet climate made it hard to keep anything dry, and food and other supplies had to be brought in from the nearest town. It was a lonely life, but Dian loved it, and she formed strong bonds with some of the gorillas.

To help identify gorillas, Dian kept records of their noseprints. The pattern of wrinkles and marks on each gorilla's nose is unique.

Dian's small camp at Karisoke has become a research center with a staff of 120 people, who work to protect gorillas.

FIGHTING THE POACHERS

The gorillas in the mountains of Rwanda were under threat from poachers. Sometimes gorillas were accidentally caught in traps, but some were killed deliberately so that their body parts could be sold. Dian was furiously opposed to poaching. She destroyed poachers' traps and sometimes she confronted the poachers directly.

UNSOLVED CASE

Dian was found murdered in her cabin in 1985. The crime has never been solved, but some people think poachers were to blame. Dian was buried in the same graveyard as some of her gorilla friends. A fund that she set up during her life still supports research and conservation of mountain gorillas.

Sylvia Earle

There is still a lot to learn about life in the world's oceans. Sylvia Earle has increased scientific knowledge by diving into the depths to explore.

Sylvia was born in New Jersey in 1935. Although her father was an electrical engineer, the family lived for a while on a farm, where Sylvia loved exploring in the nearby woods and learning more about nature. When Sylvia was 12 years old, the family moved to the Florida coast. There were salt marshes and sea grass beds near their new house, and Sylvia spent hours exploring them. After high school, she enrolled at Florida State University, where she learned to scuba dive.

QUICK FACTS

NAME: Sylvia Earle

BIRTH: 1935, Gibbstown, New Jersey

OCCUPATION: Oceanographer and explorer

EDUCATION: Florida State University, Duke University

"Every time I slip into the ocean, it's like going home. "

COLLEGE AND GRAD SCHOOL

Sylvia loved scuba diving, and she wanted to use it to study marine life. At Florida State, she decided to major in botany, the study of plants. She believed that because plants form the base of any ecosystem, the key to understanding how marine ecosystems worked would be by studying ocean plants.

After finishing her bachelor's degree, she went to Duke University to complete a master's degree and then a PhD in phycology, the study of algae.

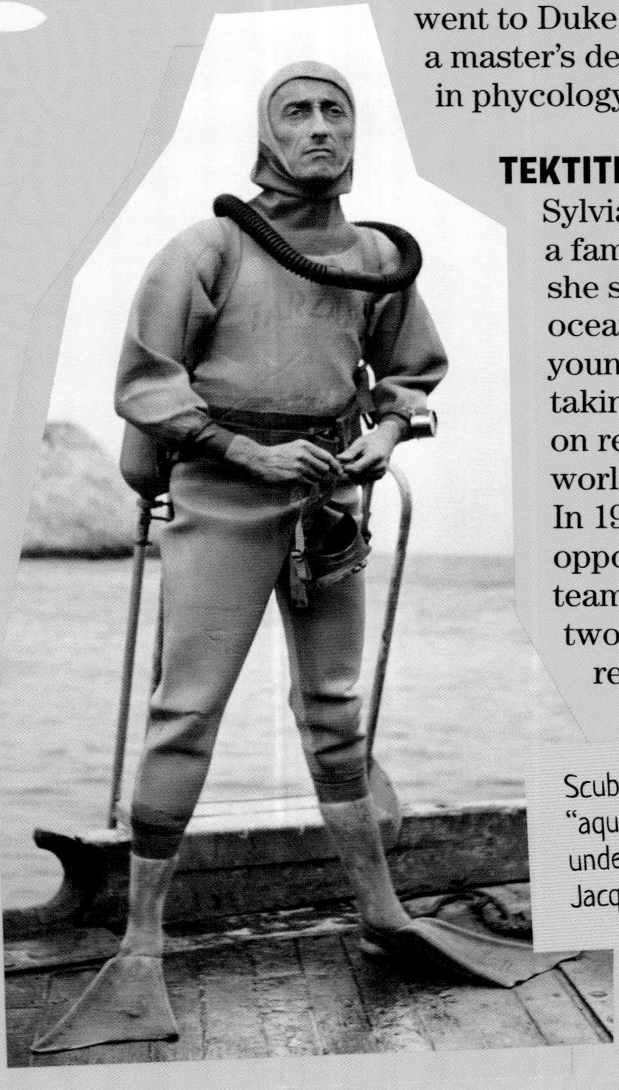

TEKTITE

Sylvia took some time off to start a family with her husband, but she still wanted to explore the oceans. While her children were young, she juggled work with taking care of them. Sylvia went on research missions around the world and spent hours underwater. In 1970, she was offered the opportunity of a lifetime: leading a team of women scientists during a two-week mission to an undersea research station called Tektite.

Scuba diving was still fairly new. The "aqualung" that allowed divers to breathe underwater was invented in the 1940s by Jacques Cousteau, pictured here.

The Tektite habitat was just off the US Virgin Islands, where the seafloor is about 50 feet (15 m) deep.

The scientists stayed underwater for the entire mission, studying coral reefs and other wildlife. They also studied the physical effects of living underwater.

SPREADING THE WORD

Sylvia's time on Tektite brought her fame. Women scientists were still the exception rather than the rule, so her team's mission caught the public's attention. She found herself in demand to give talks about ocean life and exploration. She also wrote articles for magazines and began to collaborate on books and films about marine life. Sylvia hoped that by sharing her love of the sea with the public, more people would take action to protect it.

When a diver stays deep underwater for any length of time, bubbles of gas form in their body. If the diver comes to the surface too fast, the bubbles expand like bubbles in a shaken bottle of soda. This can cause intense pain and even death.

66 **The best scientists and explorers have the attributes of kids! They ask questions and have a sense of wonder. They have curiosity. 'Who, what, where, why, when, and how!' They never stop asking questions, and I never stop asking questions, just like a five-year-old.** 99

EXPLORING THE OCEANS

Sylvia had always been a fearless adventurer, and her new fame brought opportunities. In 1979, she set a depth record that still stands today. She walked on the ocean floor at a depth of 1,250 feet (381 m) without being tethered to a boat at the surface. A special diving suit called a "JIM suit" protected her from the crushing pressure.

Ten years later, Sylvia became the first person to reach the bottom of Crater Lake in Oregon. She had cofounded a company that designed and built undersea vehicles. Using a one-person submarine called *Deep Rover*, Sylvia descended more than 1,500 feet (457 m), and used the *Deep Rover*'s pincer arm to bring up a sample of plant life from the bottom.

Sylvia's submarine was originally designed for work on offshore oil rigs. It was perfect for scientific underwater research.

For decades, Sylvia Earle has been determined to do all she can to protect the world's ocean habitats.

PROTECTING NATURE

From 1990 to 1992, Sylvia was the Chief Scientist of the National Oceanographic and Atmospheric Administration—the first woman to hold that position. Among other things, she was responsible for monitoring the health of the nation's waters. She also traveled the world to give talks about protecting ocean life.

In 2009, Sylvia founded an organization called Mission Blue. It works to make more ocean habitats protected by law. It focuses on vital ecosystems that it calls "Hope Spots."

AWARDS AND HONORS

Sylvia was named a National Geographic Society explorer-in-residence. She has also won awards for her conservation work. In 2009, she won the Rachel Carson Award, which recognizes women environmentalists. Even in her eighties, she still campaigns hard to protect the oceans.

Timeline

1758	Carl Linnaeus sets up a system for classifying living things.
1799	Mary Anning is born in England.
1811	Mary Anning discovers the skeleton of an ichthyosaur.
1817	Georges Cuvier publishes *La Règne Animal*, which describes the structure of animals both living and extinct.
1823	Mary Anning discovers a complete plesiosaur skeleton.
1837	Matthias Schlieden shows that plants are made of cells.
1847	Mary Anning dies.
1859	Charles Darwin publishes *On the Origin of Species*, detailing his theories about evolution.
1865	In experiments with pea plants, Gregor Mendel discovers the rules for passing on traits, such as color.
1890	Marjory Stoneman is born in Minnesota.
1902	Barbara McClintock is born in Connecticut.
1907	Rachel Carson is born in Pennsylvania.
1930	Using a craft called a bathysphere, William Beebe becomes the first person to observe deep-sea creatures in their natural environment.
1931	Barbara McClintock publishes her discovery of chromosome crossover.
1932	Dian Fossey is born in California.
1935	Sylvia Earle is born in New Jersey.

1947	Marjory Stoneman Douglas publishes *The Everglades: River of Grass*. Everglades National Park is founded.
1951	Barbara McClintock presents her ideas about "jumping genes."
1952	Building on research by Rosalind Franklin, Francis Crick and James Watson discover the structure of DNA.
1962	Rachel Carson publishes *Silent Spring*.
1963	Dian Fossey makes her first trip to Africa.
1964	Rachel Carson dies.
1967	Dian Fossey founds the Karisoke Research Center in Rwanda.
1969	Marjory Stoneman Douglas founds Friends of the Everglades.
1970	Sylvia Earle leads a team of women marine biologists on a mission to the underwater Tektite habitat.
1979	Sylvia Earle sets a world record for depth while diving in a pressurized suit.
1983	Barbara McClintock is awarded the Nobel Prize in Physiology or Medicine.
1985	Dian Fossey is murdered.
1992	Barbara McClintock dies.
1998	Marjory Stoneman Douglas dies. Sylvia Earle becomes a National Geographic explorer-in-residence.

Gallery

The scientists covered in this book are only a few of the women who have advanced the study of life sciences. Here are more women scientists.

Maria Sibylla Merian (1647-1717)

A German-born naturalist who became known for her beautiful illustrations of plants and animals. She applied her artistic skills to the study of insects and plants. In 1699, she was awarded a grant to travel to South America to study the insect life there. The book she published on her return made her famous.

Anna Atkins (1799-1871)

An English botanist who pioneered the use of photography in science. She used an early camera to make pictures of algae and other plants. She was the first person to publish a book that made use of photographic illustrations. She also took photos of ferns and flowering plants.

Nettie Stevens (1861-1912)

The first scientist to discover that a living thing's sex depends on its chromosomes. At the time, scientists knew that living things inherited chromosomes from their parents, but didn't understand their function. Stevens' research showed that the X or Y chromosome a living thing gets from its father determines its sex.

Marjorie Courtenay-Latimer (1907-2004)

South African museum worker who helped discover a "living fossil." In 1938, a local fisherman brought her an unusual fish, which she helped to preserve and identify. It turned out to be a coelacanth, a type of fish that was believed to have been extinct for millions of years.

Mary Leakey (1913-1996)

British scientist who studied the earliest ancestors of humans. Mary worked at Olduvai Gorge in Tanzania, searching for fossils. She discovered examples of several new species, as well as human footprints left in volcanic ash. She also developed a system for classifying stone tools.

Jane Goodall (born 1934)

The world's foremost expert on chimpanzees. She spent years studying their behavior in the wild and proved that chimpanzees were capable of using tools. In later life she campaigned tirelessly for animal conservation.

Sue Hendrickson (born 1949)

Dinosaur hunter who started her career diving for shipwrecks. She later became interested in paleontology, and in 1990 she discovered the most complete *Tyrannosaurus rex* skeleton ever found. It is now displayed in Chicago's Field Museum—and named "Sue" in her honor.

SCIENCE NOW

Not that long ago, we had little understanding of how life worked. But now we know about prehistoric life, and modern technology has allowed us to see the workings of tiny cells. New discoveries happen all the time.

Scientists are developing better strains of plants, and discovering more about how animals live. Some discoveries in genetics can be applied to the human body, and help us fight disease. And some of these discoveries are being made by women!

If you love plants and animals, and are interested in learning more about the natural world, then a career in life sciences could be right for you!

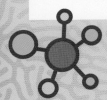

Glossary

anthropologist Person who studies the origin of human beings, as well as their societies and cultures.

botany The study of plants.

cell The smallest unit of life.

chromosome Structure found in all cells, which carries the genes that determine an organism's traits.

conservation Preserving and protecting living things from harm.

ecosystem A community of living things together with their environment.

editorial Article in a newspaper that expresses an opinion about an issue.

extinct Having died out completely.

fossil Preserved remains of a plant or animal that died long ago.

gene Tiny section of a chromosome that causes a particular trait.

genetics Branch of science that explores how traits are passed down.

ichthyosaur Type of extinct sea reptile with flippers and a dolphin-like head.

levee Embankment built to keep river water from flooding the land.

microscope Scientific tool that makes small objects appear larger.

Nobel Prize Prestigious international prize given for accomplishments in a variety of fields, including physics and chemistry.

oceanographer Person who studies the oceans and the plants and animals that live there.

paleontologist Person who studies plants and animals that lived long ago.

pesticide Chemical used to kill insects that harm crops.

plesiosaurus Extinct sea reptile with paddle-like limbs and a short tail.

poaching Illegal hunting of animals.

pollution Act of releasing harmful substances into the environment.

pressure Steady pressing force.

reproduction Process by which living things create offspring.

species Group of living things of the same type.

theory Scientific idea that is reasonable but has not been proven.

trait Characteristic or quality that makes one living thing different from others, such as hair color.

wetlands Low-lying lands saturated with water.

Further Resources

Books

Barnham, Kay. *Mary Anning (History VIPs)*. Wayland, 2017.

Fertig, Dennis. *Sylvia Earle: Ocean Explorer (Women in Conservation)*. Heinemann-Raintree, 2014.

Hustad, Douglas. *Environmentalist Rachel Carson (STEM Trailblazer Bios)*. Lerner Publications, 2016.

Ignotofsky, Rachel. *Women in Science: 50 Fearless Pioneers Who Changed the World*. Ten Speed Press, 2016.

Ottaviani, Jim. *Primates: The Fearless Science of Jane Goodall, Dian Fossey, and Birute Galdikas*. Square Fish, 2015.

Websites

Learn more about getting into STEM careers here!
www.stemcenterusa.com

Find out more about Dian Fossey' life and her work protecting gorillas.
https://gorillafund.org/who-we-are/dian-fossey/

Visit this website for more information on the Everglades!
http://www.everglades.org/

Index